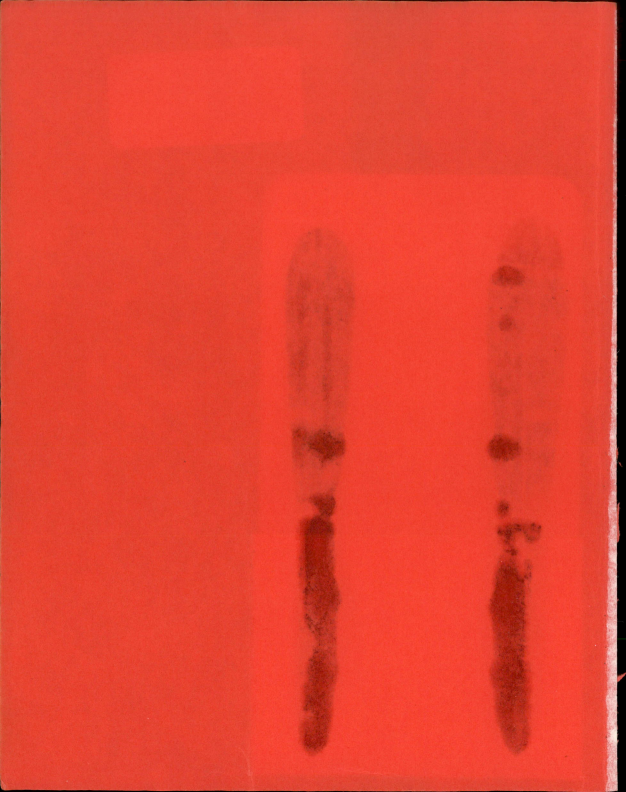

GETTING STARTED IN TENNIS

GETTING STARTED

NEW YORK 1977 ATHENEUM / SMI

IN TENNIS

ARTHUR ASHE

WITH Louie Robinson

PHOTOGRAPHS BY Jeanne Moutoussamy

Library of Congress Cataloging in Publication Data

Ashe, Arthur.
    Getting started in tennis.
    1. Tennis—Juvenile literature.   I. Robinson,
Louie.   II. Title.
GV996.5.A83   1977   796.34′22   77-5199
ISBN 689-10826-5

Published simultaneously in Canada by
McClelland and Stewart Ltd.
Composition by Connecticut Printers, Inc.,
    Hartford, Connecticut
Printed and bound by Halliday Lithograph Corporation,
    Hanover, Massachusetts
Designed by Kathleen Carey
First Edition

Contents

GETTING STARTED IN TENNIS

To My Young Friends

THERE ARE MANY reasons I wanted to write a tennis book for young players such as you.

First, such a book seems to be needed. Whenever I look in bookstores or school libraries, the only tennis books I can find are for adults. Yet I started to play the game when I was seven years old—and there were no books for me then, either. Today many more newcomers to tennis are youngsters too.

Second, sometimes it is hard to locate a person to teach you. But, if you can read, you can learn to play tennis if you have a book on the subject.

Third, young players should not necessarily learn the same way as adult players do. You are not grown up yet, so the size of the racket and the way you should play the court are different for you than they are for an adult.

My final reason for writing this book is that I have been playing tennis for 25 years now and have taken part in many tennis clinics. This book gives me the chance to pass along the many tips I have learned, and to answer many of the questions that young players have asked me.

So this book is just for you. (But if your mother or father want to improve at tennis, or learn along with you, they're welcome to read the book, too.)

WHAT YOU CAN LEARN IN THIS BOOK

The first thing to remember is, **each person must play tennis the way he or she plays best.** Don't let anyone tell you that there is only one way to play. There are many ways. Bjorn Borg, Rod Laver, Billie Jean King and Virginia Wade are all great players and they all play in different ways. This book will help you find your own way.

I suggest that you read the book carefully and then practice the things you have read. Maybe you will read the book all the way through, and then come back and work on learning a little at a time. Or you may read just a section at a time and then practice what you have read in each section. Later I'll recommend a number of specific practice techniques. Basically, you should plan on practicing for a short session every day—remembering to take a day or two off now and then—rather than going out once a week for an extra-long workout.

Another tip: **It takes time to learn anything worth learning.** When you hit bad shots, don't get upset and storm around the court wondering why they aren't coming off perfectly. Instead, think calmly about what you have read about hitting that particular shot. It is easier to try to think about a few things you are supposed to do right than a dozen things you might have done wrong. You are not Jimmy Connors, so don't be disappointed when you can't hit shots as well as he can. At this point, you don't face the opponents that Jimmy faces, anyway.

In this book I will show you several good ways to hit a forehand, a backhand, the volley and the serve, and I will also mention a little about the lob and the drop shot. There will also be helpful tips on something that is not always explained in tennis books: how to move effectively on the tennis court.

I will not teach you such shots as the topspin lob, the drop volley or a topspin backhand. As you get better, you may want to read a more advanced book on tennis or locate a teacher to show you how to hit those shots.

After we have treated the basic shots in tennis, I will tell you a little bit about strategy. Strategy is knowing where you should hit the ball in a certain situation. You may have a very good forehand and backhand, but if you hit the ball to the wrong place, you may find yourself in trouble. Strategy has a lot to do with how successfully we play this game.

This book can help you get started in what is one of the most enjoyable and fastest-growing sports in the world. You should have no trouble understanding it, for I have tried to describe things very simply. The illustrations also should help you.

(If you are a left-handed player, remember to substitute left for right and right for left in all instances given in this book.)

At the end of each instruction section, I have made up a quiz to check how much you remember of the lesson. If you don't score at least 75 on each quiz, go back and read the section again. That way you'll be sure not to miss something important.

Okay, here we go.

What You Need to Play Tennis

TENNIS IS AN easy sport to get equipped for. All you really need is a racket, some tennis balls, a pair of tennis shoes, and a court to play on.

Tennis clubs sometimes require players to wear special tennis clothes, but on a public court you can play in just about any kind of outfit. Of course, as you get better at the game, you'll probably want to dress in clothing especially designed for tennis, as it helps you feel more comfortable during play. A good tennis outfit would consist of a pair of shorts, a short-sleeved shirt, sweat socks, sweat bands for your wrists and a sweater. The sweater is more important than you might think. **Always keep a sweater on until you have warmed up, and put it back on as soon as you finish playing.** If you don't warm up slowly and cool off slowly, you risk hurting your arm, shoulder or back.

7

Now let's talk about something that your parents may not know even if they already play tennis.

Most standard tennis rackets are 27 inches long, but that is too long if you are younger than thirteen or fourteen years old. Bobby Hull or Reggie Jackson wouldn't use the same size hockey stick or baseball bat as Little Leaguers use, so you shouldn't really use the same size tennis racket as an adult. If at all possible, buy a junior-length racket, which is about 25 to 25½ inches long. If you can only find a longer one, then cut 1½ to 2 inches off the wood handle and have a sports shop position a new grip on the handle for you. The shorter racket will be much more manageable.

Another important thing to consider is price. Generally, any racket costing less than $20 is not really a very good racket, and you may be wasting your money. If you intend to play a lot of tennis, buy a racket that costs more than $20. There are all sorts to choose from: wood, metal, fiberglass, graphite and those made of combinations of these materials.

When you take a racket in your hand and swing it, it should feel comfortable to you, and you should feel you have control of it. If it feels as if it is too heavy, especially near the head where the strings are, then choose another one. **It's fine for the racket to be stiff, but it should not be too heavy to control.**

Grip size is marked on the handle of every racket. Your racket handle probably should be 4⅜, 4½ or 4⅝

Rackets are made with a variety of materials. Here are the most common types (from left to right): a standard wood racket for adults and older youths, 27" long; a composite racket, made of metal and fiberglass, also 27" long; an all-metal 27" racket; a metal racket made with a single extruded piece of metal with a "rounder" hood, 26" long; and a junior-sized metal racket, 25" long.

9

inches in circumference. I suggest that you try light-weight rackets in those three sizes before picking the one that feels the best. Unless you have very large hands, you shouldn't even pick up a racket with a 4¾- or 4⅞-inch grip. Stan Smith uses a 4⅞-inch heavy, but there are not many players of any age who can handle that.

Rackets are strung with various materials. There is a plain nylon string which stretches a lot, so that the ball does not come back off the racket as quickly when hit. There is twisted nylon, which is a little stronger than plain nylon. And then there are various types of gut strings, which are made from animal intestines. These are more expensive and usually don't last as long as nylon, but they are better to use when you become a good player because, when you strike the ball, it comes off the racket face faster and truer.

Once you have made your selection, you should **always keep a cover on your racket** when it is not in use in order to keep out moisture and to protect it from the sun and other harmful elements.

What about tennis balls? American balls, made by such companies as Wilson, Spalding, Bancroft and others, usually come in cans. When you open the can, the hissing sound you hear is air coming out because the balls are packed under pressure. They are packed that way because when each ball is made, air is pumped inside it. It is the air inside the ball that causes it to bounce. In order to keep the air inside the balls when

Smaller youngsters should choke up on their rackets if they're using adult models (ABOVE) or even if they're using junior models (BELOW). It's important to feel you have complete control over the racket you play with.

they are packed into a can, more air pressure is pumped into the can than is inside the ball. That way, air will not seep out of the balls while they are sitting in the can.

If you were to put a tennis ball recently pumped with air on a table in your room for two weeks, air would gradually seep out until the air pressure inside the ball was the same as that outside, and the ball would not bounce as high as it once did. It would be somewhat "dead."

Rackets should balance in about the middle. This junior model balances at a point that is 12½" from either end. If the racket is too heavy at the head end it will be hard to swing quickly. If it is too light at the head end it will encourage a flicky stroke rather than a smooth and solid stroke.

Other types of balls, such as the Tretorn or Pirelli brands frequently used in Europe, get their bounce, not from air pumped inside, but from the rubber of which the balls are made. The ball is thicker, and it does not bounce quite as high as the air-pressure ball. Such balls may come in boxes because there is no need to pack them under pressure since no air is pumped into them.

I would suggest that beginners start out with a box of unpressurized balls such as Tretorns. First, you get four balls instead of three. Also, these balls last a lot longer because they are a little thicker. You can't hit them quite as fast, but what you need to learn at first is control, not power, and I think you will probably learn this a lot better if you start with the Tretorn type.

As for tennis shoes, generally the more you pay for a shoe, the more comfortable it will feel and the longer it will last. But remember, at your age you could pay too much for a shoe because you could outgrow it before you wear it out.

All tennis courts everywhere in the world are built to the same dimensions. In my view, youngsters such as you should start playing on a **smaller** court than this, because you cannot possibly cover all the shots in tennis the way older and faster players can. I think a court that is approximately four-fifths the size of the standard tennis court, with a net that is 37 or 38 inches high near the sidelines rather than 39 inches, would make it easier for twelve-year-olds and younger—and also for senior

13

If you reach out as though to shake hands with your racket (ABOVE) you'll automatically assume a good grip on the handle, with fingers spread on the grip for greater control and with the racket parallel to the ground. A hammer-type grip (BELOW) should be avoided because it reduces control over the racket and sets the racket face much too high for hitting ground strokes.

citizens—to learn and to enjoy the game.

Maybe these changes I advocate will not occur in the near future. Chances are most youngsters will still have to learn to play the game on the standard-size court. Bear in mind that as you mature, though, the court will not seem so big or the net so high. That will help you overlook the frustrations of chasing balls now at the start of your progress in the game, and concentrate on the fun parts.

Okay, slip on your tennis shoes, pick up your racket and a box of balls, and let's go out to the tennis court.

Lesson #1:
The Forehand

WE START our lessons with the forehand stroke rather than with the serve, because when you go out to the court to warm up, the first thing you do is bounce the ball off the ground and hit a forehand to your opponent. It is just natural to use your "fore" hand or dominant hand (right hand if you are right-handed) to start things off.

The illustrations in this chapter show good forehand form. The backswings and follow-throughs may be slightly different for different players, but in the hitting zone—that foot-long area where the racket meets the ball—the strokes look almost exactly the same.

Okay, now that you've taken a look at the ways the forehand can be made, take your racket out of the cover and hold it in front of you so that it points outward from your stomach and you are looking at the edge, or rim, of

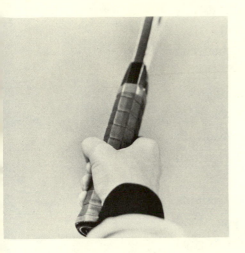 

To grip the racket for the forehand stroke, put your hand on the handle so that the V formed by thumb and first finger is lined up along the right edge of the top panel on the racket. Notice that this puts the meaty part of your hand behind the racket when you hit.

the racket. The forehand grip is made by spreading your fingers along the handle so that the V formed by your thumb and forefinger is positioned on the right top edge of the handle. This permits you to make contact with the ball with as much support as possible from your hand.

Now you can hit a forehand using the **loop backswing,** in which the racket is brought back past your face in a loop and then straight through the ball, ending up with the racket following through somewhere between your left shoulder and your head. Or you can hit the forehand using the **straight backswing,** with the racket being brought straight back—not looped—then straight forward along the same path.

17

At this point, **the important thing to remember is your grip and keeping your eye on the ball. Also, finish your swing with the racket somewhere between your left shoulder and your head.**

Ideally, when the ball comes toward you over the net, you should turn your body slightly sideways to the right so that you see the ball more with your left eye than your right eye. As you bring your body back on the backswing, you should find it turning naturally by itself.

The point of contact for the forehand is roughly that narrow area between both hips as you stand sideways to the approaching ball. You want to start making contact about the time the ball reaches your

The best spot to meet the ball with the forehand stroke is at a point opposite your belly button.

right hip and keep the ball on the strings until the racket reaches your left hip. You have a little leeway here for your own individual stroke, but these two points should be kept in mind.

The most important thing now is to **hit the ball in the middle of the strings. Disregard where it goes, because even if you hit the ball solidly and it goes over the fence, this is a good beginning.** It is just a matter of time and experience before you learn how to control the ball's flight.

A natural feeling to look for in hitting the forehand is, **from your windup through the follow-through, your body weight should be shifting forward from your right foot to your left foot as the racket swings from behind you on through the hitting zone to the desired point between your head and left shoulder.**

CORRECTING FAULTS	**The two biggest faults in hitting the forehand are: (1) not taking the racket back in time, and (2) not following through.**

Many beginners hit the ball too late. **By the time an opponent's shot bounces, your backswing should be complete. You should be ready to begin the forward part of your stroke as the ball bounces.** Try using a rhythmic count of one–two, starting just as you bring the

1

2

In these pictures of a forehand stroke, the player takes her racket straight back (Figs. 1 and 2) rather than in the looping arc some players prefer. Notice how well she moves her weight onto her front foot (Fig. 3) and finishes with the racket high, pointing to the top of the back fence (Fig. 4).

racket back, to set up a smooth, well-timed swing. Remember, the word "rhythmic" should tell you this is **not** a quick, jerky count. Also make sure you bring the racket back all the way in one continuous sweep and swing it forward in the same manner.

The second biggest fault among beginners is that, when they feel the racket against the ball, they stop the stroke without a follow-through. Remember, you must not finish your stroke until the racket reaches a position between your head and left shoulder.

One thing you must realize is that you cannot afford to be lazy on a tennis court if you want to play well. Laziness can cause you to hit the ball late and into the net. The ball goes into the net because the player really does not get up to it in time to hit it at about waist level.

If you are hitting the ball too long, there may be a couple of causes. You could be hitting the ball too early, or you could be shifting your weight before your follow-through. But with experience you should correct this. Remember, the object is to hit the ball between the court's boundary lines, not to see how hard you can hit it.

FOREHAND QUIZ

Score 12½ points for each correct answer. A perfect score is 100.

1. *What are the first two things you want to think about as a beginner on the court?*
2. *What is the correct finishing, or follow-through, position for the forehand stroke?*
3. *What is the point of contact, or "hitting zone," for the ball?*
4. *How high should the ball be on the bounce when you hit it?*
5. *What area of the racket face should contact the ball?*
6. *How should your weight shift as you contact the ball?*
7. *As the ball approaches you, where should your racket be when the ball bounces?*
8. *What are the two biggest faults of beginners hitting the forehand?*

ANSWERS

1. *Your grip and keeping your eye on the ball.*

2. *Somewhere between your left shoulder and your head.*

3. *Between both hips as you stand sideways to the ball.*

4. *Waist high.*

5. *In the middle of the strings.*

6. *From your right foot to your left foot.*

7. *At the end of your backswing, ready to begin your forward stroke.*

8. *Not taking the racket back in time, and not following through.*

Lesson #2:
The Backhand

THE BACKHAND STROKE is so called simply because, as you swing your hand toward the ball from the left side of your body (or right side if you are left-handed), you are almost literally hitting it with the "back" of your hand.

The difficulty with the backhand is control, because all you have behind the racket when you contact the ball is your thumb and less than half of your hand. The hand is turned a quarter inch or so on the handle so that the V formed by thumb and forefinger straddles the **left** edge of the handle. Thus, **timing is actually more important in the backhand stroke than in the forehand,** because the power and control that you get on the backhand comes, not from a strong grip, but from timing. So **it is essential that you develop a lot of racket-head momentum and**

To get power, it's important to meet the ball earlier on the backhand side than on the forehand side. Always try to hit the ball before it gets past your front foot.

make contact with the ball in front of your right foot.

The swing itself is an upward motion. **You want to bring the racket back as low as is comfortably possible—past the left hip is a good place to start it from—and sweep your arm in an upward motion, ending high and wide.** But remember, the point of contact must be in front of the right foot. If the ball gets past

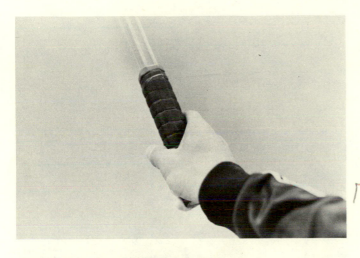

In the backhand grip, the V formed by thumb and first finger is lined up along the left edge of the panel on top of the racket. That puts more of the thumb behind the handle for greater control.

27

1

2

3

4

In these backhand pictures, the player shifts side-on to the ball as he takes the racket straight back, then moves his weight forward, into the shot, and follows through high. Holding the racket with two hands instead of one hand helps many youngsters control shots better on the backhand side. It's worth using the two-handed grip if you're having trouble swinging the racket one-handed, or if your backhand shots lack any power.

your right foot into the area of your belly-button or left foot, you are in trouble.

Contact the ball with your weight shifting from your left foot to your right foot (just the opposite of the forehand), and follow through with your arm sweeping high and wide. At the finish, the elbow of your right arm should point directly at the fence along the right side of the court.

One fault many beginners make on the backhand is carrying the elbow of the hitting arm too high as they prepare to hit the stroke. This is an attempt to compensate for a weak wrist, and women and juniors are especially guilty of it. It causes you to sling your racket at the ball in a sidespin-producing motion. Practice keeping your elbow down as you begin to time the ball better. Chris Evert is a good example of a top player who hits the ball with her elbow down. The same is true of Borg and Connors and Laver—and Ashe.

As with the forehand, another key fault in the backhand is not getting the racket back in time to make the stroke. If you don't get the racket back in time, you're going to hurry the shot.

BACKHAND FAULTS

Many players weaken their backhand strokes by allowing the elbow of their hitting arm to collapse as they stroke through the ball. If you try not to let the wrist get too far ahead of the racket hand when you swing, you won't make this mistake.

BACKHAND QUIZ

Score 20 points for each correct answer. A perfect score is 100.

1. *What is the most important thing in hitting the backhand?*
2. *What is the contact point for the ball with the backhand?*
3. *From what racket position should you start the backhand?*
4. *How should your weight shift as you strike the ball?*
5. *What are the two most common faults in hitting the backhand?*

ANSWERS

1. *Timing.*
2. *In front of your right foot.*
3. *Somewhere near the left hip.*
4. *From your left foot to your right foot.*
5. *Carrying the elbow too high, and not getting your racket back in time.*

Lesson #3:
The Volley

A VOLLEY IS a shot hit before the ball touches the ground on your side of the net. The correct grip to use to volley is neither the forehand nor backhand grip, but the continental grip. The V formed by thumb and forefinger is positioned exactly at the center of the top panel. With this grip, you can volley balls hit to your left or your right side.

The big differences between the volley and ground-strokes (forehand and backhand) are:

1. In the ready position for the volley, instead of the racket being parallel to the ground, the head of the racket is cocked upward so that the head of the racket is in line with your eyes.

2. On the forehand volley, you must bend the wrist outward as you stroke, and on the backhand volley you

When you're up at net looking for a chance to volley, remember to hold the racket head high, as shown, and to place your free hand on the throat of the racket as an aid in moving the racket to the forehand or backhand side when you spot the ball's direction.

must bend it back toward your body. On the forehand volley, the wrist bend is similar to one you would use in preparing to catch a ball thrown to you. On the backhand volley, the wrist bend is like one you would use in slapping someone next to you with the back of your hand.

The length of the volley stroke is quite short with little

34

or no backswing involved. The stroke is on a down and out path, which permits the racket to impart underspin to the ball.

Never let the racket get behind you when volleying. Keep it in front of you, and the earlier you hit the ball, the better. **Hold the racket a little tighter because the ball is traveling roughly twice as fast at the net as it is when it gets back to the baseline.** Also, keep your elbow as close to your rib cage as possible. You don't want your elbow flying off into space during a volley.

VOLLEY FAULTS   The major technical fault made in volleying is swinging the racket across the body, rather than in a downward motion under the ball and out toward the net.

Most faults in volleying are psychological. Players tend to flinch at net because they are scared or nervous. They have not psychologically mastered the volley position. **When you get to the net, you are in command, and when you see the ball coming you must go after it. You must approach the volley as if you are in control of the situation.**

When you flinch, the racket head is usually dropped below the wrist, and you end up hitting the ball into the bottom of the net. **The racket must be kept cocked up at eye level.** With the ball traveling at increased speed,

35

1

2

3

The volley is a short stroke with little or no backswing. The first moves
(Figs. 1 and 2) should be toward
the oncoming shot. The sooner you
meet the ball, the more weight
you'll put in the shot and the sooner
it will get back over the net. The
finish (Fig. 3) shows that the stroke
has been made with the racket head
sliding under the ball. This puts
underspin on the shot for greater
control. Notice where the player's
left hand is in Fig. 2. He's really
using that free hand to keep the
head of the racket from going back
too far and getting behind his body.

hand and eye coordination must be keener. Actually putting the racket near eye level not only helps with this, but also gives more support to the shot when the ball is hit.

VOLLEY QUIZ

Score 12½ points for each correct answer. A perfect score is 100.

1. *What is the correct grip for the volley?*
2. *Where do you hold the racket to be ready to volley?*
3. *What should your wrist do on the forehand volley?*
4. *What should your wrist do on the backhand volley?*
5. *What must you **never** do with your racket in the volley?*
6. *Should you grip the racket tighter or more loosely when you volley?*
7. *How do you make contact with the ball in the volley stroke?*
8. *How should you **feel** when you are at the net to volley?*

ANSWERS

1. *The continental grip.*
2. *Cocked upward directly in front of you at about eye level.*
3. *Bend outward.*
4. *Bend backward.*
5. *Let it get behind you.*
6. *Tighter.*
7. *A short stroke downward and outward toward the net.*
8. *You should feel that you are in* **command** *of the situation.*

Lesson #4:
The Serve

A GOOD DEAL of your success in tennis will depend on how well you serve, so it is important to develop a toss-and-service motion that works for you.

There are two grips for serving. The forehand-type grip gives a wide-open racket face to the ball when you swing it from your shoulder. The more advanced backhand-type grip gives a more closed racket face to the ball and so produces more spin and control in the long run.

The beginner should start serving with a forehand grip. Stand on the baseline near the center service mark with the intention of placing the ball in the opposite service court.

To begin your serve, put your racket on your shoulder, and place the ball in the tips of four fingers

39

In first learning to serve, put the racket on your shoulder before making the toss. That will make it much easier to coordinate the two actions of lifting the ball and swinging the racket.

of the left hand. Your little finger should not touch the ball. (If you are under twelve, do not put any fingers on the ball at all, but simply hold it in the palm of your open hand.) Now, **facing the right net post, start your left arm up to toss the ball, holding the arm straight out— but not stiff—and move it in a line straight up the net post. At the same time, your right arm should be**

40

bringing your racket back and up. The two arms start this motion together.

The toss should begin with your weight on your right foot, and when you release the ball you should start your weight forward onto your left foot as you prepare to hit the ball.

The ideal toss is one which puts the ball at a height you can reach with your arm and racket fully ex-

The best toss is one which puts the ball at a height you can reach with your arm and racket fully extended.

41

Here's the proper starting position for the serve once you've gotten the knack of coordinating ball toss with swing. The ball is held lightly in the fingertips and the racket is cradled comfortably on the wrist of the tossing hand. It's important to stay nice and loose—relaxed—for the serve because it requires more rhythm than any other stroke.

As the ball is released, the racket is taken back in a natural manner similar to that used in winding up to throw a baseball.

Just before the ball begins to drop, reach up and forward and hit through it with your racket. Finish the stroke with your right foot inside the baseline. That forward step is very important. It makes you toss the ball far enough in front.

tended. Just before the ball begins to drop, reach up and hit through it with your racket. Finish the stroke with your right foot inside the base line.

Trial and error will teach you how fast to hit the ball and how to get it across the net into the proper service court. Once you achieve this, you will have mastered the beginner's serve.

As you become a more experienced player, you can

43

switch to the backhand-type grip, or continental grip, to serve. With the more closed racket face caused by these grips, greater spin is put on the ball.

In first learning to serve, don't hit the ball into the corners or near the sideline. Simply try to get it across the net and into the proper court.

Also, never toss the ball up while you are shifting your weight backward. Only toss it while your weight is leaning forward.

If you are under twelve and have been tossing the ball with an open palm as we suggested, you can begin to improve your toss after playing awhile by learning to hold the ball in your fingertips.

If you find yourself hitting the ball into the net, chances are you are not tossing the ball high enough into the air over your head when you serve. This causes you to bend your elbow too much and swing with a cramped arm motion. Toss the ball nice and high, perhaps just a bit higher than you can reach with your racket.

SERVICE
FAULTS

If you toss the ball too high, however, you will have to wait for it to come down, and this will delay and weaken your serve.

You may also find that, although you are tossing the

44

ball up and a little into the court in the direction of the right net post, it seems to be arcing back toward you. The problem may be that you are holding the ball in the palm of your hand and, as the ball rolls off your fingers, which curl inward, it tends to travel on an arc back toward you. The ball has started out in the right direction, but has arrived at the wrong place.

The body works better when both arms work together. In tossing the ball and winding up your racket for the serve, try to coordinate these movements.

SERVE QUIZ

Score 15 points for each correct answer. A perfect score is 105.

1. *Which racket grip should a beginner use to serve the ball?*
2. *Where should your racket be placed to begin the serve?*
3. *What point should you face to begin the serve?*
4. *How should your weight shift as you toss the ball into the air?*
5. *How high should you toss the ball?*

45

6. *If you hit the net when you serve, what is one possible reason?*

7. *Do the arms work together or separately when you serve?*

ANSWERS

1. *The forehand grip.*
2. *On your right shoulder.*
3. *The right net post.*
4. *From your right foot to your left foot.*
5. *As high as, or just a bit higher than, you can reach with your racket.*
6. *You did not toss the ball high enough.*
7. *Together.*

Lesson #5:
Footwork in Tennis

BEFORE YOU CAN hit the ball, you have to get to it—on all shots in tennis except the serve. And that involves footwork. Even if an opponent hits a ball right at you, proper footwork must be used to make your return stroke.

Ilie Nastase and Evonne Goolagong represent the ultimate in grace and footwork on the tennis court. They are so athletically coordinated that they just seem to float across the surface.

For purity in footwork preparation, one has to point to Ken Rosewall. He is seemingly always in position. That's because he moves so quickly to get to the ball.

Efficient, smooth weight shift is what makes Goolagong, Nastase and Rosewall look so graceful. Flow is another word for effective weight shift. It's something that originates in good footwork, and it has to be learned.

Good footwork does three things:

1. It enables you to shift your weight from your rear foot to the front foot, thereby transferring your body weight to the ball as you swing.

2. It helps you maintain balance (if your footwork is correct and you practice it, you will find you will be much more balanced than someone who does not know the correct techniques of footwork).

3. It helps your coordination.

Let's examine these three elements in more detail.

Weight Shift

If you don't shift your weight from the back foot to the front foot, you're really spinning your wheels. You're not using your body to the best advantage, so it is not working efficiently. When you **do** shift your weight, you don't have to swing at the ball as hard because your body is doing most of the work.

Until you learn how to coordinate this weight shift from the back foot to the front foot as you move through the hitting zone and before the ball leaves your racket strings, you really won't look like a smooth tennis player.

Ideally, you want to keep the ball on your strings as your weight is shifting from the back foot to the front foot when making the stroke. When the ball leaves your racket strings heading for the other side of the net, your weight should then be on your front foot. When you finish either a forehand or backhand—with the racket high and wide—you should swing around, pivoting on the left foot for the forehand and on the right foot for the backhand. In so pivoting, you will be swinging your weight around to a balanced, ready position for your next stroke.

It is easier to shift your weight if your knees are slightly bent, because this gives you a low center of gravity.

The best way to achieve the proper weight shift is to concentrate harder during the time you make contact with the ball. That is, try to look at the ball harder, try to keep your knees bent a little bit longer, and resist the urge to look up before the ball leaves your strings. As your weight is shifting through the stroke, keep your eye on the area of the strings. You know where the ball is going to go, so don't worry about it; in time, you can hit a ball into the correct part of the court almost blindfolded.

Basically, when you look up, you are trying to see if you have hit a correct shot; but you are taking your eye off the ball and hitting an incomplete shot, one in which the ball does not stay on the strings long enough.

Balance is really everything when it comes to looking good on the tennis court. Some players, when they finish a stroke, look as if they are about to fall flat on their face, or flat on their backside.

If you set up wrong when you hit the ball, you're off balance when you complete your stroke, and that's proof

A balanced ready position is the starting point for getting to each ball quickly and efficiently in tennis.

At the baseline (LEFT), awaiting serve or taking up your position between shots, your knees should be bent, weight centered on the balls of the feet, and racket held comfortably in front of the body, pointing at the net.

The ready position is the same at net (BELOW) except that the racket head is held much higher. That makes it easier to hit down on the ball with your volley stroke and also speeds up your reactions because the racket is at eye level.

that you've done something wrong. Usually, the problem is that you are standing "too tall." If you remember to bend the knees and keep the body weight closer to the ground, you will be in a more stable position.

Think of it this way: If you stood straight up with your knees locked without any flex at all and your hands down by your sides, someone pushing against your shoulder would be able to knock you over rather easily. However, if you were to spread your legs a bit, bend your knees and put your arms out like a defensive guard in basketball, you could resist a push several times stronger than the first one.

The correct body position for balance (as you quickly get into position with your good footwork) at the end of the forehand stroke is for your right arm to be between your left shoulder and your head. But where should your left arm be? Well, your left arm should be extended a bit to counterbalance you when your right shoulder is pulled way around. If you put your left hand into your pocket and really swing at a forehand, you are liable to fall on your right shoulder.

Try it. Not so hard that you actually fall, but just enough so you get the sensation of what is called "centrifugal force" pulling you not only around, but down. If you try hitting the backhand with your left hand in your pocket, the feeling is that you will not be able to stop unwinding yourself.

If your legs are spread out sufficiently when you finish

These pictures show an effective use of body weight in the forehand stroke. Early on the backswing (Fig. 1), the weight is on the back foot. As the racket nears the ball (Fig. 3) the weight moves onto the front foot, to make sure enough power will be put into the shot. In the balanced follow-through (Fig. 4) the racket has swung around high and wide and the player is ready to move into position for his next shot.

Notice how the backswing shown here is different from the backswing in the forehand pictures you saw earlier. This player takes the racket back in a looping arc, whereas the player shown before takes the racket straight back. Both styles are effective. It's up to you to choose the one you like best.

your stroke, if your knees are bent and you've stayed low throughout the whole shot, and if your left arm is extended a bit to counterbalance that spinning effect of the backhand or falling down on your right shoulder on the forehand, then you won't feel awkward when you finish the stroke.

Coordination

I saved discussion of coordination for last because if you do the two things I just mentioned—shift your weight and maintain your balance—you will automatically achieve coordination. Weight shift plus balance equals coordination.

But let's say you are shifting your weight but you're not balanced. This usually happens if you are standing too tall (knees not flexed) at the beginning, middle or end of the stroke. Or, you are maintaining your balance but not shifting your weight. Then your arm will have to try to make up for the work your body should have done, and you will end up swinging too hard. When you swing too hard, you cannot stay balanced and therefore you become uncoordinated.

In moving to hit a ball coming onto your side of the court, you want to "skip" to the ball. That is, from the **HOW TO MOVE ON THE COURT**

54

ready position, with your weight forward on the balls of your feet, you "skip" sideways—without your legs crossing each other—until you get to the ball. Then you move your left leg past your right to hit the forehand, or your right leg past your left to hit a backhand.

Remember to keep your knees slightly bent rather than straight and stiff. Also, you should always try to keep your weight a little bit forward on the balls of your feet or your toes. If you rest your weight on your heels, you may easily find yourself suddenly off balance.

You will have to learn much of proper movement on a court through trial and error, by trying to do it right and looking out for your own mistakes. Remember, it takes as much patience to learn the game of tennis as it does to learn to read or solve math problems. Some things may not come as easily as others at first, but if you keep trying, one day a particular movement will suddenly feel right and you will see the results. Practice makes perfect.

How to Play a Game ...Set...Match

IF YOU HAVE BEEN watching tennis matches on TV or at your local park, you probably already know that the object of the game is to hit the ball into your opponent's court in such a way that he or she (1) cannot reach it to return it, or (2) hits it back into the net or outside the boundary lines. Each time that happens, you earn one point. The first player to score four points with at least a two-point advantage wins a game.

However, tennis has a somewhat different method of scoring. It is traditional rather than logical. Each time you win a point, it is not recorded or credited as a point. The first point either side wins is recorded as "15," and the player having no points, instead of being said to have zero, is recorded as "love." Thus if the person serving scores the first point, the score at that time is called

"15–love." Since the server's score is always called first, if his opponent scores the first point, the score is called "love–15." The second point scored by either player is credited as "30," but the third point, when added to the first two points, gives the player a total of "40," rather than "45," as logic would seem to demand. On either of the first two points, if the score becomes tied it is then called "15–all," or "30–all," but if the score becomes tied with each player having 40, the score is referred to as "deuce," and a player must score **two consecutive points** (that is, two in a row) to win the game. If he scores one point, the game is said to be at his "advantage," or "ad," meaning he now has the best chance to win because if he scores the next point it is his game. But if that player's opponent scores the next point, the game is returned to deuce.

The player serving first stands to the right of the center line and behind the baseline of what is called the forehand, or "deuce," court (the left side is called the backhand, or "ad," court). The serve is made over the net into the opposite service box.

Here are the main rules you need to know to play the game.

SERVING

1. You get two chances to put the ball in play. If your first try hits the net but lands in the proper service court, it is called a "let" and you get to start over,

57

||still having two chances. If your second serve hits the net and goes in, you get one more chance. **Every time you hit the top of the net with your serve and it goes in, you start again with that serve.**

2. If your serve strikes the net but does not go across into the proper court, or if your ball clears the net but lands outside the proper court, it is called a "fault," and you are allowed but one more try. If you fault on your second try, that point goes to your opponent.

3. You cannot step into the court before you hit your serve. That is called a "foot fault." Your feet must remain either behind the baseline or in the air until you hit the serve. You are allowed to jump, but you cannot back up two feet or more and get a running start. A foot fault counts the same as a fault.

4. If you toss the ball up to hit it and you miss, that counts as a fault because you **tried** to hit it.

5. If, when playing doubles, you hit either of your opponents with your serve before the ball touches the ground, you win the point. If you hit your partner while serving doubles, it is a fault if you do it on your first serve; it is a "double fault" (and you lose the point) if you do it on your second serve.

6. You can serve any way you like (overhand, under-

58

arm, sidearm), as long as you hit the ball before it hits the ground.

7. If you break a string in your racket while serving a fault, that's bad luck for you. **It is not treated as a let.** However, if something happens on the court between your first and second serves that is not your fault and it delays the game, you are allowed to serve your first serve again.

8. You cannot serve until your opponent is ready to return.

RULES FOR PLAY

1. You must hit the ball on **one** bounce or while it is still in the air from your opponent's racket.

2. If the ball hits any part of you or your clothing, you lose the point. You may use the racket only—any part of it.

3. You change sides of the net with your opponent after the first game of **every** set, and then after every two games. When in doubt, add up the total number of games played in a set and if it is an odd number (one, three, five, seven, etc.), change sides.

4. When you play a tie-breaker at six games each, change ends after every six points.

5. If a ball bounces or rolls onto your court from another court, you can play the point over again. If

59

a ball drops out of your pocket or that of your opponent, you can play the point over only if both players agree to.

6. In doubles, after every set you and your partner may change the order of serving. That is, whoever served first in the last set may now serve second if you so desire.

7. When playing without an umpire, be fair, and if you are not sure where the ball landed, play the point over again.

8. In tournaments, you are not allowed any coaching until the match is over.

After either player scores the first point, the server then moves from the right to the left side of the court and serves again, and he continues to alternate from side to side after each point is scored, serving the entire game. His opponent then serves the second game in the same manner. The games are continued until a player (or a team in doubles) wins six games, which makes him the winner of the "set." Players may play a "match," with the winner being the first player to win two sets (two out of three), or the first player to win three sets (three out of five).

In playing sets, however, if the players become tied at five games each, one of them must win two games in a row to win the set. If a player wins but one game and then his opponent wins the next, tying the games at six—

all, then they play what is called a "tie-breaker."

There are two kinds of tie-breakers: (1) sudden-death tie-breakers, and (2) the 12-point tie-breaker.

There are two types of sudden-death tie-breakers. In the 13-point tie-breaker, the first person to score seven points wins the set. At six–all, the next point is "set point." In the nine-point tie-breaker, the first player to score five points wins. At four–all the next point is "set point."

With the nine-point tie-breaker, players take turns serving two points each for the first six points, after which the next server gets to serve three points in a row.

In the 13-point sudden-death tie-breaker, the first server serves one point, and then the players alternate, serving two points each until the set is over.

This is also true of the 12-point tie-breaker system. In a 12-point tie-breaker, the first player to score seven points with a two-point advantage wins the set.

Tie-breakers are used whenever a set is tied at six–all.

For a complete set of the official rules of tennis, write: U.S. Tennis Association, 51 East 42nd Street, New York, N.Y. 10017.

Conduct on Court

TENNIS IS A game of true sportsmanship, and as such there are rules of etiquette—or conduct—which must also be observed.

The rules of etiquette for the game of tennis should really be divided into two sections: (1) your attitude and actions toward yourself, and (2) your attitude and actions toward your opponent and the public.

Your attitude about yourself has to be your first consideration, because how you present yourself, how your opponent sees you, and how the public sees you, if anybody happens to be watching, has a lot to do with the way you will play, and it will go a long way toward determining how people think of you when you are out there playing, whether it's in a public park or a private club.

First, you should always be clean. Your clothes, even

if they are simply cut-off jeans instead of a regular tennis outfit, should be neat and clean. The same is true of your shoes, even if they are not white tennis shoes.

In general, you want a neat appearance because that's the way the sport is. And if you form these good habits while you are young, you will keep them as you grow older.

You also want to think about how you would like to be treated if you are going out to test yourself against somebody else in a sport such as tennis. You would not want your opponent to cheat you, or not try against you, or not really prepare for a serious match. When you finish a match, whether you were just practicing or playing in competition, you want to feel that you have had fun, gotten a lot of exercise, done your best, and want to come back and do it again.

As for your attitude toward your opponent, first of all, you must realize that the most important thing about the game of tennis and you at this stage of your life—more important than whether you win or not—is that you have fun. You are not always going to win and you are not always going to lose; you will do some of both. But if you are doing serious practice or competition, you want to know that you were prepared well and you did your best, and that you got your share of the fun of the game. And this is the attitude you should have toward your opponent. If **he** starts screaming and yelling and throwing his racket, keep **your** cool.

Another rule is, be on time. You probably do not like to be kept waiting and you should not keep your opponent waiting. If you make an appointment to play at two o'clock, be there at ten minutes to two. The rule is: It is impossible to be on time if you are not there ahead of time. It most often takes a few minutes to get ready and get onto the court anyway.

Once the game starts, in the absence of linesmen and other officials, make sure you call things as you see them. If you are not sure about how a ball lands, say "Play a let." This is one way in which tennis differs from other sports—a point is sometimes replayed if there is doubt about which way it went. On a clay court, if a ball leaves a mark when it strikes near the base line, you can tell if it was in or out. But on a hard surface, where the ball does not leave a mark, then you have to take an educated guess and be very careful how you call it.

Also during the game, you should always—but **always**—call out the score after every point. That way, there should be no confusion later on as to what the score is.

If there is any doubt in your mind about something regarding the game, ask your opponent; he is not your enemy, he is out there to have fun just as you are.

Remember at all times that your opponent deserves just as much consideration as you do.

And it is considered a mark of character and good

sportsmanship always to shake hands with your opponent after a match.

Now, whether you are playing in a tournament before an audience, or in a public park—which everybody's tax dollars help to pay for—with people watching, you must be courteous to those looking on. There must be no profanity, no racket-throwing, no intentional hitting of balls against the fence.

It's natural to get upset if you miss an easy shot. The problem with getting angry is, once you do it the first time, it gets worse and worse. It becomes easier to get mad the second time, and this time you are usually more angry than you were the first time. It just keeps building up and usually while it does, you start to lose. You may notice that if you miss a shot and then hit a ball into the back fence in anger, you will often end up missing the next **two** shots because you are still worrying over the first shot you missed. Think about it.

What you want the public to know when you come off the tennis court is that you had a lot of fun, played well, and are a credit to the community and the sport.

To sum it up, here are some final pointers:

1. Appearance:

Most people wear tennis outfits, though you don't have to. At a public park you can wear anything— almost. But you can, if you feel like it, purchase an

inexpensive tennis outfit at any department store or
tennis shop.

2. When playing:

a. If a ball from another court rolls onto your court but
does not disturb you, finish your point and then
return your neighbor's ball. If the ball does roll into

*Keeping your court tidy and free of
litter such as empty ball cans and
soda bottles are simple ways of observing good tennis etiquette and
making the game more enjoyable
for all players.*

66

the playing area, **don't get angry:** just return the ball and play the point over.

b. If you are playing with new balls purchased by your opponent or partner, offer to pay half the cost.

c. Don't ever call your opponent names or curse at him. Calling him a ''cheat'' is the worst. If you don't think he plays fair, don't play with him anymore. **Always be fair. Cheating is never acceptable! Never!**

d. Always get off the court when your time is up. Usually courts are reserved an hour at a time, so when your time is up, leave.

e. Don't walk **behind** your neighbors' court when they are playing a point. Wait until the point is over.

f. Always leave the court as you would like to see your own court left. Pick up all your trash—old tennis cans, pop bottles, etc.

g. In general, during a match, keep your comments to yourself. Don't laugh at your opponent if he misses an easy one or brag about your great forehand.

67

Lesson #6:
More Strokes to
Help You Win

NOW THAT YOU have tried the forehand, backhand, volley and serve, here are a couple of more strokes for you to learn—but only after you have gained some familiarity with the first four.

The important thing about hitting the lob is to get set by planting your back foot so that as you stroke the ball, you are leaning forward. You want to get under the ball and hit it up in the air as high as you can with an upward sweeping stroke and your racket facing the sky. THE LOB

A young player might use the lob quite a bit on a clay

68

The lob is a shot played when you're caught behind your own baseline and the opponent has moved up to net. The stroke is made by getting under the ball and hitting it in the air as high as you can with an upward sweeping action, and with the racket face pointing toward the sky.

court to keep opponents as far back as possible. Chances are, if you hit a deep lob, unless your opponent returns with the same kind of shot, you would have an excellent opportunity to hit a drop shot on your next stroke.

Ideally, your lob should drop somewhere between the service line and the baseline. If it drops anywhere in there, you are in great shape. You also want to hit it as high as possible because the higher you hit it, the straighter it will drop down. You may hit it up at an angle, but a very high lob will still drop straight down, and a ball dropping straight down is very difficult to hit. In fact, if such a ball is hit to you, be sure to let it bounce before you attempt to return it.

The time to hit a nice high lob is when you are chasing a deep ball hit by your opponent and he is coming to the net.

THE DROP SHOT

The strategy behind a very young player (thirteen years old or younger) hitting a drop shot is not to win the point, but to pull his opponent off to one side of the court, thereby leaving the other side open.

Never try a drop shot from the baseline, not even if you go on to become a professional player some day. **Only try a drop shot if your opponent has hit the ball within your service court,** which means, as far as he is concerned, you are probably coming to the net to hit an approach shot (a shot you will hit back down the sideline and then come to the net).

The reason I say "never" is because the margin for error is too high. You are likely to hit the ball into the net, or make it easy for your opponent to hit back a point-winning stroke.

The element of surprise is all-important when hitting the drop shot, and you have to be able to hit it when you are in control of the shot.

The technique in hitting the drop shot as far as a young player is concerned is simply to think about how hard you have to hit the ball to get it just over the net. Don't think about how you are going to do it; how you do it will be dictated by your mental picture of the power the shot will require.

QUIZ FOR LOB
AND DROP SHOTS

Score 15 points for each correct answer. A perfect score is 90.

1. *What is the most important thing in getting set to hit a lob?*

2. *In which direction should your racket face as you hit a lob?*

71

3. How high should you hit a lob?

4. Where should your lob land?

5. How should you hit a drop shot?

*6. When should you **never** hit a drop shot?*

ANSWERS

1. Planting your foot back so that you can lean forward as you hit the ball.

2. Toward the sky.

3. As high as you can.

4. Between the service line and the base line.

5. Any way you can to get it just over the net.

6. From the baseline.

Lesson #7:
Strategy

ONCE YOU HAVE learned to hit the basic shots in tennis, you need to start thinking about where and when to hit those shots so that you can win over your opponent—who might be able to hit those same shots just as well as you can.

Outplaying an opponent of equal or better shot-making ability involves what is known as strategy, and that is what we are talking about now.

By far, the majority of points are won on errors made by your opponent, rather than by you making great shots. So, basically, the longer you can keep the ball on the court, the better your chances of winning the point. Bear that in mind as you consider these fundamentals of winning tennis strategy.

1. When you are serving, **try to get two out of three**

of all your first serves in. At your age, don't expect to serve aces (a dazzling first ball that your opponent can't hit back). All you want to do is develop a consistent serve, and if you can get two out of every three serves inside the service court at this stage of your learning, you will be really preparing yourself well as you grow older and stronger.

2. If you do commit a fault while serving, try to make that fault by hitting the ball **over** the service line rather than **into** the net (even though the results are the same as far as your opponent and the score are concerned). The reason is this: **It is much easier to learn to let up a little bit on your serve than to speed up.** If you hit your first serve long, then you just hit your second one a bit easier. If you hit your first serve into the net, you still haven't gotten to the ball park yet, and a little bit stronger on your second serve may still not be enough to get it over the net, while a lot stronger may be too much.

3. **You should work toward building a good, sound spin service.**

4. If you are serving and the score is 15–all, 30–all or 15–40 (on this latter, your opponent is one point away from winning the game), **serve the ball down the middle.** It's safer that way. Don't open up the court by trying to serve wide to your

opponent's forehand.

5. If you are serving and the score is 15–love, 30–15 or 40–love (you're ahead on all of these), you might **try serving the ball real wide.**

6. When you get into a rally, **get the ball back into the court four times before you even think about winning the point.** If you will do that at your age against opponents of about the same age, I firmly believe you will win almost every match you play. It sounds simple, but remember this: **Most people, especially juniors and beginners, tend to make an error within the first three shots.**

7. **Don't even think about hitting an approach shot to the net unless the ball bounces within the service court.** If the ball bounces between the service line and the baseline, stay in the back court. If you are going to hit an approach shot and come to the net, unless your opponent is way off court, **hit the ball down the line.** Then come in and expect your opponent's shot to come back down the same line. That is, come in and stand a little bit left of center if you hit your backhand down the line, and if you hit your forehand, come in and stand a little bit right of center. This means you actually concede that part of the court that you have left open. If your opponent can actually put a ball past you into that part of the court, then

he has really hit a fine shot. But you have the percentage part of the court (the part where the ball is mostly likely to come) covered like a blanket.

8. You should never consider hitting an approach shot cross court unless your opponent is just way off court and you have that part wide open. **It is very dangerous to hit an approach shot cross court.**

9. **When in doubt about what to do in the back court, hit a nice, deep ball down the middle.** You can't hurt yourself with that.

10. At your age, **don't think about trying to win the point on a return of your opponent's serve.** Remember the rule of getting the ball safely into your opponent's side of the court four times before trying to win the point. Winning it on return of service comes in three or four years, when you are stronger.

11. If your opponent is a net-rusher, make sure that if he wins the point, you don't lose it. That is, **don't try some spectacular passing shot that you might miss.** Let your opponent go ahead and volley the ball. He may be able to hit a shot that you will miss, but **he** might miss while trying to.

12. If you find yourself trailing your opponent by quite a lot during a match, it is undoubtedly because you have been making too many errors.

76

Therefore, if you are already observing the rule of getting the ball into the court four times before trying to win a point, **increase that number to five, thereby increasing the margin for your opponent to make an error.** Learn to play more error-free tennis, because at every level of skill in tennis, matches are seldom really won; instead, they are lost—lost by the player who makes the most mistakes.

Exercises

PROFESSIONAL TENNIS PLAYERS—and young players would do well to follow this example—find it best to limber up before they even walk onto a tennis court. If at a single court, we usually run around the court four times. If there are two courts side by side, we run around the pair of them twice.

Tennis is a very strenuous activity, and if you just walk onto the court and start running after tennis balls, it is like getting up in the morning and running a 440-yard dash. **You must warm up your body first for five minutes.**

Most players get to play at most courts for one hour at a time, so your body should be warmed up through exercises before you go on the court to play. This way, you won't spend valuable minutes of the hour just warming up your body. But most important, by exercising before you walk on the court, you make it much less likely that you'll get a cramp, sprain an ankle or develop soreness in shoulder or elbow.

In addition to taking a pre-game run around the court, try this series of exercises too:

1. Stand with your hands on your hips and just roll your head in one direction for about 15 seconds. Then roll it the other way for 15 seconds.

2. With your arms at your sides, roll your shoulders forward and down and back up again for 15 seconds. Then roll them backward, then up, back and around for 15 seconds.

3. Stand with your feet shoulder-width apart and swing your arms in the same directions that you rolled your shoulders. Do this for 15 seconds in each direction.

4. Now, swing your arms back and forth horizontally. Swing them around as far as they can go! Do this for 20 seconds.

5. Stretch the back muscles used for serving by standing with the feet a shoulder-width apart, extend both arms into the air and grab your left wrist with your right hand and slowly pull your left arm over your head. You should feel your left side stretching. Pull as far as you comfortably can and hold it for 5 seconds. Then return both arms to extended positions in the air. Repeat this again, but this time

Tennis is such a strenuous activity that it's wise for all players, young or old, to warm up for at least five minutes prior to a match. Exercises limber up the muscles—and they're fun to do.

you should be able to pull the left arm a little more. Hold it in that position for 5 seconds and then return to the straight-up position. Now switch, grabbing your right wrist with your left hand and repeat the exercise.

6. Now for the legs. First, stand with your feet together and reach down as far as you can with both hands and hold there for 5 seconds. Come back up and shake your legs. Repeat, but this time go down farther with your hands; hold for 5 seconds. Come back up and repeat a third time, making sure to **go as far as you can this time,** and hold for 5 seconds. Shake your legs.

7. Sit on the floor and extend the left leg, but bend the right leg around so the right heel is close to your right thigh. Then with both arms try slowly, very slowly, to reach your left toes. Do this two or three times and then switch legs.

8. For the last exercise, jump up as high as you can 10 times. **Now your body is warm. Let's go out and play some tennis!**

Court Surfaces—
What's on Top
Counts

ONCE YOU HAVE learned how to play the game of tennis, you should take a closer look at the court surface you're playing on.

There are various surfaces for outdoor courts, and different ones for indoor courts. But there are really only two different surface characteristics: Clay courts and then all the hard courts.

The ball bounces a lot faster on the hard courts, and the height of the bounce depends roughly on what is in the sub-soil. For instance, Dynaturf is a hard surface often used indoors. It has a thin layer of cork that makes you feel a little like you're walking on mashed potatoes and causes the ball to bounce higher than, say, Laykold, another hard surface. That's because the Dynaturf surface with its layer of cork gives a little and shoots the ball back out a bit.

Clay courts "give" because clay is made of dirt, and dirt is compactible. That is, it compresses a little bit and shoots the ball back. The big difference in playing on clay is that you have to learn to slide, which you can't do on hard or synthetic surfaces. **Most of the time on clay courts you will be hitting the ball at waist level or above, and you have to learn to slide into your shots so that when you come to the end of your slide, you are executing the forward part of your swing.** Then you regain your balance and move back to the desired part of the court. **Because of the sliding on clay, accuracy becomes more important than speed, so you might want to string your racket a little more loosely** so that when it contacts the ball, the ball will stay on the racket strings a little longer.

If you are playing on a hard or asphalt-type surface, you should try playing with tighter strings because in this case speed is more important than control. On these surfaces, the ball comes at you a lot faster.

Clay is seldom found now as an indoor court surface because it is difficult to maintain inside. Therefore, if you play indoors you are more likely playing on Dynaturf, Laykold or Sportface (which is pretty much like a rug).

Outdoors you will probably play on Laykold or a clay surface. There are three other common terms for clay: (1) composition, (2) Har-tru, and (3) *En-tout-cas,* a French

84

term which, roughly translated means "in all cases," literally meaning an all-weather court. But a clay court is a clay court.

Practice for Fun and Improvement

WHILE PLAYING tennis matches is fun, in order to really improve your game, you must practice, and that should be fun, too. Many people do not like to practice because they think of it as work or just drudgery. But there are games you can play while practicing. And remember, while you are practicing, you are improving.

It is not the number of hours a day you practice that is important. It is what you do while you are out there. **Practice, except when you are playing practice matches, should be specific.**

Usually, if you are going to take a day to practice, it should be divided into two parts. The morning session should be limited to trying to improve some one shot on which you believe you are weak. You may hit forehand volleys, then you may hit backhand volleys for 20 minutes each. Then you may serve two buckets of balls (about 50 serves). You may also want to practice your quickness. If a friend wants to serve to you, you may want to simply practice your preparation for the return of service. You may want to conclude the session by a little rope-skipping, or sit-ups or some other exercise.

Then cool it for a while.

In the afternoon, you can come back and play matches or some other sort of competitive game. You can play an ordinary set with conventional scoring, or you may play an 11-point game in which the same person serves until he wins 11 points on his own serve. In this game it does not matter how many points your opponent gets. You keep serving until your own total reaches 11. Next your opponent takes over and serves until he wins 11 points. Then you can compare scores on who had to hit the most serves to win the 11 points. This can really take a long time, but you will get plenty of practice in serving against an opponent.

You can play 21- or 31-point matches, with each player serving five times in a row. And you can play the same game another way: If you want to improve your concentration on return of service, you can play that whoever wins the most points while returning service wins the match. (Jimmy Connors or Ken Rosewall would be great at this because they have great service returns.) This forces you to really concentrate not to miss that return of serve, which is usually caused by trying to go for a winner off the return. Usually the game-winning total in this exercise is set no higher than 11 points.

You definitely should not practice every day. Every now and then you should take two or three days off. This does not mean that you particularly need physical rest. Go swimming or play baseball or golf. Just don't play tennis. Get away from it for a while. During this period you might think about the game, however, reviewing fundamentals in your mind, spotting your weaknesses and the cause of them, and deciding what to practice next.

Danger signals, particularly in hot weather, include dizziness and nausea. **If you feel yourself getting dizzy in the head or sick in the stomach, stop immediately.** Your body is telling you something: You are not physically equipped at this stage in your preparations to continue.

Watching tennis tournaments on television can be instructive, but I don't think you should watch shots so much as note what certain players do in particular situations and at certain stages of the match. Pay attention to such things as when players hit an approach shot, whether they hit an underspin or a topspin backhand, what kind of serve they hit when down love–30, where they serve, and when a player chooses to lob.

You can also learn a lot about what not to do. You may see a player get burned trying a cross-court approach shot and losing the point.

Certain players can be watched for certain strokes, but there is a danger in trying to copy what someone does just because he is a good player. As I said earlier, there are many different winning styles in tennis. Your style may not resemble the one you see on TV and therefore you would not benefit from emulation of it.

A great way to learn while watching televised tennis is to take the statistical approach: **Chart the match.** Take a piece of paper and make five columns with the headings: serve, forehand, backhand, volley and overhead. Do this for both players. Now all you have to do is keep track of the errors made with these strokes. A pattern will develop quickly. A player's weaknesses will become glaringly evident. Once they do, watch to see how he or she tries to compensate for them, and how his or her opponent tries to exploit them.

Make two more columns for each player at the bottom of the page. In one, mark down the number of points won because of an unreturnable shot. In the other, mark the number of points won because of an opponent's error. At the end of the match, compare the two columns, and you'll discover in virtually all matches 90 percent of the points are lost rather than won. The conclusion is obvious. To be a winner, you must cut down on the number of errors.

Watching a televised match may not improve your game as much as practice can, but it can point out the aspects of the game which you need to work on. So next time you're home watching a match and somebody calls and asks what you're doing, don't say you're watching TV, say you're taking a lesson.

Eating Right
Is Important

WHAT YOU EAT and when you eat is important if you want to play good tennis.

Your stomach empties in about an hour and a half. You should therefore try to eat from two to two and a half hours before playing a match.

What you want to eat before a match are foods called carbohydrates. These include rice, spaghetti, potatoes, bread, etc.

Carbohydrates are to muscles what gasoline is to a car. Your muscles cannot "run" without them, because your muscles burn glucose and glycogen, of which carbohydrates are made.

You may have a great-looking, finely tuned body, but if there are not enough carbohydrates in your system, your muscles won't work as well as they should.

After you have played a match, your body actually loses cells, and these cells are rebuilt with foods known as protein, which help build a strong body and maintain body weight. Excellent sources of protein are lean meat, fish, eggs, cheese and yogurt, among others. Protein is to your body what a motor is to a car.

Milk is always one of your best sources of good nutrition, but you should have it after the match. Stay away from dairy products before a match, because if you get nervous or upset, they curdle in your stomach.

Remember to balance your meals with vegetables and salads and fruit.

About half an hour before a match, try to drink as much liquid as you comfortably can. Then, sip a little bit of water or Gatorade every time you change court ends. One or two mouthfuls should be enough. You want to maintain a certain water level in your system throughout the match. Gatorade is pleasant-tasting and better than water because it is a balanced solution of water, sugar (containing the glucose your body needs) and salt (sodium), all of which the body burns at a balanced rate.

If you play tennis on a very hot day, take a salt tablet after two sets. This will prevent cramps.

Getting Serious
about Tennis

AFTER YOU LEARN the fundamentals of tennis and you begin to play reasonably well, you may move into intermediate and, later, even advanced stages, through more reading, more practice, and more lessons.

If you decide to become serious about the game—that is, to be better than the average player—there are four things you should do.

1. Get the best equipment that you can afford.
2. Take as many lessons on technical development and strategy as you possibly can.
3. Having done the first two, start playing in as many competitive situations as you can—local tournaments, whatever. **It is how you are able to perform under pressure that will improve your level of expertise in the game.**

4. Play doubles, too. Doubles play is not only fun, but a great way to get more experience hitting lobs, volleys, and overheads. It teaches you the value of getting your first serve in, and familiarizes you with the style of play up at net.

The first thing you look for in a teacher is whether he or she is a member of the U.S. Professional Tennis Association, which is an organization of men and women who teach tennis for a living. The address of USPTA headquarters is: P.O. Box 145, Wakefield Station, New York, N.Y. 10466. If your teacher is a member, you can be sure he or she is a capable one. But you also should try to find out if this particular teacher is good with younger players. Some teachers are excellent with youngsters but not so good with adults, or it may be the other way around. Some teachers, excellent though they may be in teaching tennis, do not have the patience necessary to deal with very young players.

If you are twelve or thirteen years old and thinking about becoming a professional tennis player, you should concentrate on being the very best you can in junior competition in the various age groups, because that is the training ground for professionals. The junior ranks continually feed our professional ranks. The major junior competitions around the world are in Kalamazoo, Michigan (the U.S. National Juniors) and, the most important of them all, the Orange Bowl in Miami.

If you have done very well in playing in tournaments

in your region, then you should try to get an invitation to play in the Orange Bowl. This tournament brings together the best junior players from all over the world. Some of the past winners of the Orange Bowl include Rod Laver, Tony Roche, John Newcombe, Harold Solomon and Billy Martin. You will know how well you stack up against other young players your age as a result of how well you do in the Orange Bowl. If your entry is even accepted into the Orange Bowl, you are pretty good.

Exposing yourself to the best competition wherever you can is very important. Just do well in your own age division and the rest will take care of itself.

If you are ten years old and you aspire to be a professional tennis player, you will know in the next five years, probably, what kind of chance you have. If you have good equipment and good instruction and do not find yourself among the top players of your age in competition in the region where you live, then the chances are against your making it as a tennis pro. But if you are keeping up with your age group regionally and nationally, please continue to work to become a pro.

Generally, you need to be in good physical condition. **The one thing physical conditioning gives you more than anything else is confidence.** If you know that you are in better shape than your opponent, then you will be comfortable putting the ball in four times before you make a mistake because you know you have the staying power to hang in there and outlast the other player. It's also very frightening psychologically to your opponent the next time you play him: He knows that not only did you beat him, but you outlasted him, you wore him out. You came off the court fresh and he was nearly exhausted.

Another thing: It is not how fast you run the 100-yard dash that matters in tennis; **it is how fast you run 20 yards.** You have to be quick rather than fast, for in tennis, quickness counts more than sheer speed.

Remember also that you do not need brute strength. Timing is the thing. Strength can only help up to a point, and past that it gets in the way. Some players tend to think that if they are strong enough, they can simply muscle the ball and they won't take time to master the fluidity necessary to get great timing. **Simply trying to overpower opponents does not make a championship tennis player.**

There is more to the game of tennis than just winning or losing, however. It is, in fact, a very character-building experience. From the very beginning, you should **practice total honesty on the court.** To begin with, tennis is a one-on-one sport—and at your level there will be no linesmen in most cases, except when you are playing in tournaments—and you will be calling your own lines. That is, on a ball hit close to the lines, you must call whether it is in or out. If your opponent hits a ball past you and it touches the line, you must have guts enough to call it "good." Otherwise, you cannot expect him to do the same in return.

If you start to play competitive tennis early, you will find yourself among people from all walks of life, from different cultures, of different races, speaking different languages. More than anything else, you should take advantage of the wonderful opportunity to acquaint yourself with these differences so that you will become more comfortable with them as you grow older.

There is no room for ethnic, racial, class or economic prejudices in tennis. Tennis players come in all shapes, sizes and colors from all over the world, and in the locker room, they are all the same. Rod Laver, an Australian who is one of the best players the world has ever seen, may find his locker next to a player who had to qualify to enter a tournament. He doesn't have a special room, he doesn't get extra time on the massage table, he doesn't get preferred treatment in the shower or the dining room or anywhere else. He may be seeded, but once the tournament starts he is treated just like everybody else. And that's the way it should be.

Glossary of Terms

ACE: A point-winning service struck so well that an opponent fails to even touch it or attempt a return.

ACROSS COURT: A shot played diagonally across the court from one corner to another; also termed "cross court."

AD-IN, AD-OUT: Scoring expressions meaning advantage-server and advantage-receiver during a game that has reached deuce.

ALLEY: The lane between the singles sideline and the doubles sideline; not in play in singles.

AMERICAN TWIST: A serve in which the racket strikes the ball with an upward and sideward motion, causing the ball to spin and take a high bounce, usually to the receiver's backhand.

APPROACH SHOT: Usually a shot played from inside the

service court, behind which the striker advances to the net position.

BACKSPIN: Spin applied to the ball by hitting down behind it, causing the ball to rotate in the opposite direction it travels.

BASELINE: The back line at either end of the court.

CANNONBALL: A hard flat serve.

CENTER MARK: The mark bisecting the baseline, defining one of the limits of the service position.

CENTER SERVICE LINE: The line dividing the right and left service courts.

CHANGE OF PACE: Altering the speed and power of shots.

CONTINENTAL GRIP: Used by some players for forehand, backhand and volleys. Sometimes called the service grip.

CROSS COURT: See "Across court."

DEFAULT: To lose a match by not playing or by stopping before the match is completed.

DEUCE: A scoring expression used when players are tied after the fifth point in a game. One player must then score two successive points to win.

DOUBLE FAULT: When the server fails to put either of the two serves allowed for each point into the correct court. A point is then awarded to his opponent.

DOWN THE LINE: A shot hit to the same side of center from which it is hit.

DRIVE: A shot hit after the bounce with a full stroke.

DROP SHOT: A shot hit with underspin to land short on the

other side of the net.

EASTERN GRIP: The most common grip for holding a racket.

FAULT: A served ball that does not land in the proper court or is not properly served.

FOOT FAULT: Standing inside, or putting a foot inside, the baseline before a served ball is struck.

FORCING SHOT: A shot played from the baseline forcing the opponent on the defensive and eliciting a weak shot or an error.

GAME POINT: A point which will give one player the game.

GROUND STROKE: A stroke made after the ball is allowed to bounce.

HALF VOLLEY: A shot hit just barely after it has hit the ground.

HEAD: The frame and strings of the racket.

LET: A served ball that touches the net but goes into the proper court. Also any stroke that does not count and is played over.

LOB: A ball that is hit high into the air and lands in the opponent's backcourt.

LOVE: A scoring term meaning zero, or nothing. It is derived from the French word "l'oeuf," which means egg. When the game was taken up in England, the French word was pronounced "love."

MATCH POINT: The point which, if won by the player who is ahead, wins the match. Double match point is when the score is 40–15 or 15–40 in a match game, and triple match point is when the score is 40–love or love–40 in a match game.

NET: The netting stretched across the middle of the court.

NET GAME: A type of strategy in which a player attempts to reach a position in the front court in order to utilize volleys and overheads to win points.

NO MAN'S LAND: An area midway between the baseline and the service line in which a player should not stand while awaiting an opponent's ball because it will most likely be at his feet.

NOT UP: A call made when a player fails to play the ball before the second bounce.

PASSING SHOT: A ball that passes an opponent at the net.

PLACEMENT: A successful shot that an opponent cannot reach; usually a ground stroke.

POACH: A play in doubles in which a player at net crosses into his partner's half of the court to volley the ball.

POINT: A single score. Four points scored wins a game unless both sides have three points—thus the score is deuce—and one side must then score two consecutive points to win.

RALLY: A long series of shots in which both players are able to keep the ball in play.

RANKINGS: A listing of players according to their performance of the previous year.

SCRAMBLING: When a player is able to keep the ball in play regardless of correct technique.

SEEDINGS: The listing of players in a tournament on the basis of recent performances.

SERVICE: The act of putting the ball into play.

SERVICE BREAK: When the server fails to win the game he serves.

SET POINT: The point which, if won by the player who is ahead, wins the set.

SIDELINE: The line at either side of the court that marks the outside edge of the singles playing service.

SLICE: A ground stroke or volley hit with backspin.

THROAT: The part of the racket where the head joins the handle.

TIMING: The rhythm that produces a perfectly hit shot.

TOPSPIN: Spin applied to the ball by hitting through the ball from low to high, causing the ball to rotate in the same direction it travels.

TOUCH: The delicate feeling some players develop for striking the ball or executing certain shots.

TWIST: A type of serve hit with topspin.

UNDERSPIN: See "Backspin."

VOLLEY: A stroke made by hitting a ball before it has touched the ground, except in serving.